Unearthing Your Purpose

Through discovering your God given abilities

Mary-Ann Oyejobi

This book is published by
Grosvenor House Publishing Ltd
Link House
140 The Broadway, Tolworth, Surrey, KT6 7HT.
www.grosvenorhousepublishing.co.uk

A CIP record for this book
is available from the British Library

Paperback ISBN 978-1-83975-997-0
Hardback ISBN 978-1-83975-998-7

Acknowledgements

First and foremost I would like to give thanks to God Almighty for giving me the ability to complete this book, and for placing within my mind such a wonderful vision to create. The Lord's great wisdom has enabled me to bring this God-given dream into reality, and for this I am grateful.

I would like to express my sincere gratitude to my understanding family, who have always surrounded me with a vast amount of love, prayers, support and encouragement. Thank you Dad, Mum, Debbie, and Anna. I love you all very deeply and I thank God for your lives.

I would also like to acknowledge the members of Noah's Ark Sanctuary Church for all their assistance over the years. I also recognise and appreciate the contributions which several individuals made towards the launching of this book; God bless you all.

Many thanks go to Caroline and Eric, for investing their time, energy and effort in proofreading my work, and for giving me sound constructive criticism.

Once again, I would like to give special thanks to God for helping me successfully accomplish this project. I praise the Lord for surrounding me with Spirit-filled, positive, thoughtful and inspiring individuals who have helped me on this special journey.

Opening

The intention of this book is to help individuals along their journey of living out their God-given purpose, by pointing them back to the Bible. This is to ensure that they are directed by biblical truths throughout their decision making. The word of God is not only a guide but a source of encouragement for all during moments of difficulties. This is because we can be reminded of God's written promises through reading and meditating upon Holy Scripture. This book also requires readers to participate in a variety of activities. These tasks have been designed to help individuals live out their purpose through taking active steps. To fulfil our purpose we must be intentional about the choices we make, and strive to turn wise ideas into practical achievements.

This book is a guide and is NOT meant to replace the Bible or God's spoken word to you. It does not have ALL the answers, but we serve an awesome, loving God who knows ALL things.

It is my prayer that you accept the wisdom of the Holy Spirit, and allow Him to guide you along your journey to fulfilling your purpose. Amen

Love from
Mary-Ann

Contents

Imitate Christ

Do not let your past or present circumstances, race, gender, age, upbringing, class, or your location of living, be an excuse to not achieve your purpose! Christ was born during a time when the Jewish race, alongside many other conquered peoples, was living under Roman dictatorship. During the Roman Empire many individuals lived in oppressive communities with very limited rights. Christ's family was not the wealthiest of families, and Jesus was usually referred to as '*just* the carpenter's son'. But He did not allow unfavourable circumstances, or unproductive criticisms, to stop Him going to the cross. Everyone has a purpose in life; Christ's purpose was to save mankind through His death and resurrection (**Luke 13:32**). Jesus KNEW who He was, He KNEW He was the Holy Son of God, and He did not allow the negative opinions of others to determine who He was. And neither should you!

Matthew 13:55 *Then they scoffed, "He's just the carpenter's son, and we know Mary, his mother, and his brothers—James, Joseph, Simon, and Judas.* (NLT)

Matthew 16:13–17 *When Jesus came to the region of Caesarea Philippi, he asked his disciples, "Who do people say that the Son of Man is?" "Well," they replied, "some say John the Baptist, some say Elijah, and others say Jeremiah or one of the other prophets." Then he asked them, "But who do you say I am?" Simon Peter answered, "You are the Messiah, the Son of* *the living God." Jesus replied, "You are blessed, Simon son of John, because my Father in heaven has revealed this to you. You did not learn this from any human being.* (NLT)

Luke 13:32 *Jesus replied, "Go tell that fox that I will keep on casting out demons and healing people today and tomorrow; and the third day I will accomplish my purpose.* (NLT)

So, when you hear comments such as:

- You are *just* an undergraduate.
- You are the *only* one who I know trying out something like this, therefore there is a high probability that your plan will not work out. Are you sure you want to do this? (A way in which the seed of doubt is sown.)
- You are *only* young. Just wait till you are older. (A potential way in which you can delay doing what God has called you to do.)
- You are *just* a single lady. You do not need to pursue such dreams at your current point in life. In fact, women should not do such things at all.

You must learn to respond in a godly manner ... For example, 'I am a child of God with an extraordinary purpose, and my existence is necessary to mankind because my God says so. Therefore, I choose to follow God's instructions concerning His will for my life.' Or remain silent instead of responding in anger.

John 1:12 *Yet to all who did receive him, to those who believed in his name, he gave the right to become children of God.* (NIV)

Believe you are who God says you are

Moses focused on the fact that he had a stammer, yet God saw him as a deliverer, someone who could lead the nation of Israel out of Egypt.

Exodus 4:10–13 *But Moses pleaded with the* L*ORD, "O* L*ORD, I'm not very good with words. I never have been, and I'm not now, even though you have spoken to me. I get tongue-tied, and my words get tangled." Then the* L*ORD asked Moses, "Who makes a person's mouth? Who decides whether people speak or do not speak, hear or do not hear, see or do not see? Is it not I, the* L*ORD? Now go! I will be with you as you speak, and I will instruct you in what to say." But Moses again pleaded, "Lord, please! Send anyone else."* (NLT)

Gideon was concerned about his clan being the weakest of his tribe. Yet the Lord saw a warrior in Gideon, a warrior fit for battle.

Judges 6:15 *"But Lord," Gideon replied, "how can I rescue Israel? My clan is the weakest in the whole tribe of Manasseh, and I am the least in my entire family!"* (NLT)

Sarah thought that she was too aged to have a baby, but God saw Sarah as a mother of many nations. Sarah in her old age gave birth to her son Isaac, the promise child.

Genesis 18: 12-14 *So Sarah laughed to herself as she thought, "After I am worn out and my lord is old, will I now have this* *pleasure?" Then the LORD said to Abraham, "Why did Sarah laugh and say, 'Will I really have a child, now that I am old?' Is anything too hard for the LORD? I will return to you at the appointed time next year, and Sarah will have a son."* (NIV)

Jesus KNEW who He was (He is God in flesh appearing). He knew where He was going (His purpose was to go to the cross and to save the world from sin). He lived according to the word and fulfilled written prophecy concerning Himself. Christ is the Messiah, the Saviour of the world.

John 8:14 *Jesus told them, "These claims are valid even though I make them about myself. For I know where I came from and where I am going, but you don't know this about me.* (NLT)

God has the power to elevate you regardless of how lowly or insignificant you may 'feel'. Remember our feelings do not always reflect reality.

God's approval is ALL you need

You do not need approval from a group of elite individuals for your work efforts to be deemed relevant or useful. This is because, if God has called you to do it then God has already approved your work. God SEES you and He NOTICES your endeavours! You are approved by the Holy Spirit and recognised by the Creator of the Heavens and the Earth.

You do not need accreditation from an exam board to prove your worth, and neither do you need an OBE to show your value. You are of great value and significance because the blood of Jesus says so.

Your existence does not need validation from another human being. The fact that you were born, delicately woven together in your mother's womb, is your validation for existence. That is your evidence that you are of value to the world! You are valuable. You can show another human being kindness, and present others with the gift of love, even if it is only for a moment. This act alone is invaluable.

Your talents, gifts and purpose may seem insignificant to others, but if you are doing what God has called you to do then you are living the BEST life and putting a smile on the Lord's face.

Many individuals refused to accept Christ for who He was, but Christ did not let this stop Him from achieving

His purpose. Their approval meant nothing to Him, for He knew He was the Son of God regardless of what others said about Him.

John 5:39–41 *"You search the Scriptures because you think they give you eternal life. But the Scriptures point to me! Yet you refuse to come to me to receive this life. "Your approval means nothing to me.* (NLT)

Write your vision down, make it plain to see

Habakkuk 2:2 *Then the LORD said to me, "Write my answer plainly on tablets, so that a runner can carry the correct message to others.* (NLT)

Sometimes there is a need to write information down as this can help bring about clarity with regards to what you plan to achieve in the future. It can also serve as a reminder and a form of encouragement, making clear how far God has brought you along your journey to fulfilling your purpose.

Purpose: The reason as to why something is done or created, or for which something exists.

Goal: An aim or desired result.

Dream: A *cherished* aspiration, ambition or ideal.

Gift: A natural ability or talent.

Getting to know your purpose

1. How to know your purpose: Ask the Holy Spirit (PRAY ABOUT IT).
2. What to do when you are confused about your purpose: Ask the Holy Spirit for help, guidance, direction and wisdom (once again, PRAY ABOUT IT).

Never fall into the trap of underestimating the power of prayer, for the prayer of a righteous person produces marvellous results.

You do not have to do anything to get your gift (natural ability) as it is something which God has bestowed upon you. You can grow it and work on it, but you do not have to do anything to receive it, for it is already within you. Your purpose is connected to your gift and understanding WHY you have a gift can help aid you in discovering what your purpose in life is.

Take a few minutes right now to pray to the Lord to give you clarity on WHAT He has called you to do, WHEN He requires you to act, and HOW He wants you to act.

Questions

1) What do you find yourself consistently desiring to achieve throughout life?

....
....
....
....
....
....
....
....
....
....

2) What strengths do people highlight about you during conversations?

....
....
....
....
....
....
....
....
....
....

3) List all the things which hold great importance to you in life, e.g., principles, people, places etc.

....
....
....
....
....
....

....
....
....
....

4) List your strengths.

....
....
....
....
....
....
....
....
....
....

5) List some of your passions and interests.

....
....
....
....
....
....
....
....
....
....

6) What do you truly want to achieve in life?

....
....
....
....
....
....

....
....
....
....

7) How can your strengths, values and passions help you achieve your purpose?

....
....
....
....
....
....
....
....
....
....
....
....
....
....
....
....
....
....
....
....

Extra writing space can be found in the appendix

Some practical tips

To discover what abilities/gifts you have stored within you, you need to TRY things out. For example, you will never know that you are a great actor if you do not try acting. The same goes for every other vocation. So...

- Sign up for clubs/classes or enrol on a course (strive for continual personal development).
- Mix and interact with different groups of people.
- Go out into the world and taste things. It's from the varying experiences we encounter that we get to know ourselves better and discover new interests, likes and dislikes.
- Own the interests you love regardless of whether others share your passions. Even if people dislike what you do, what is truly important is that you are following your God-given heart's desire.
- Spend time with family members and friends who engage in different activities.
- Network, network and network some more. Meeting with others provides the opportunity to learn and grow from different people's experiences.

Glorify God in all you do

A major point which I desire to highlight is that you do not have to run a ministry to live out your God-given purpose. You can honour God through your nine-to-five job; after all, the time a person spends at work will consume a large proportion of their life. You must remember that you can glorify God through your career as a cleaner, hairdresser, nail technician, footballer, retail assistant, healthcare worker, accountant, etc. Strive to do your best wherever The Lord has placed you and learn to be content in the place in which He has positioned you, for godliness with contentment is *great gain.*

Colossians 3:22-24 *Slaves, obey your earthly masters in everything you do. Try to please them all the time, not just when they are watching you. Serve them sincerely because of your reverent fear of the Lord. Work willingly at whatever you do, as though you were working for the Lord rather than for people. Remember that the Lord will give you an inheritance as your reward, and that the Master you are serving is Christ.* (NLT)

1 Timothy 6:6 *Yet true godliness with contentment is itself great wealth.* (NLT)

Not everyone will share the same vision as you

Not everyone will approve of your goals, this includes family, friends and church members! People may even suggest that you should give up and try something different. Some may even question whether you have heard from God or not. Do not feel disheartened or dismayed. Multiple people doubted that Christ was the Messiah. Many even challenged Him with regards to who He thought He was and felt insulted when He referred to God the Father as His Father. Even Jesus' own brothers did not believe Him.

John 7:3–5 *And Jesus' brothers said to him, "Leave here and go to Judea, where your followers can see your miracles! You can't become famous if you hide like this! If you can do such wonderful things, show yourself to the world!" For even his brothers didn't believe in him.* (NLT)

Even though many individuals disbelieved Christ's claim to be the Son of God, this did not cause Christ to change His view of Himself. He knew the truth and held onto it.

John 8:25 *"Who are you?" they demanded. Jesus replied, "The one I have always claimed to be.* (NLT)

Remember that in order to achieve, all you need is God's presence and His go-ahead.

Judges 6:16 *The LORD said to him, "I will be with you. And you will destroy the Midianites as if you were fighting against one man."* (NLT)

It can be extremely frustrating when individuals do not understand you or your goals, but do not allow feelings of frustration to control you. Learn to handle such matters in a godly fashion by using gentle words to diffuse a person's anger. For example, Gideon encountered conflict due to acting on God's instruction to him. Gideon used wise words to avert unnecessary drama. This shows me that, although we may do exactly as The Lord requires, others may take offence. Gideon's fellow Israelite men argued heatedly with Gideon with regards to how he handled the process of events that took place.

Judges 8:1-3 *Then the people of Ephraim asked Gideon, "Why have you treated us this way? Why didn't you send for us when you first went out to fight the Midianites?" And they argued heatedly with Gideon. But Gideon replied, "What have I accomplished compared to you? Aren't even the leftover grapes of Ephraim's harvest better than the entire crop of my little clan of Abiezer? God gave you victory over Oreb and Zeeb, the commanders of the Midianite army. What have I accomplished compared to that?" When the men of Ephraim heard Gideon's answer, their anger subsided.* (NLT)

Always remember that a gentle answer diffuses anger, so be wise, loving and kind with your words.

Proverbs 15:1 *A gentle answer turns away wrath, but a harsh word stirs up anger. (NIV)*

It'll get tough

In this life we will face several challenges and the Bible states that many are the afflictions of the righteous. But the Lord will deliver him/her from them ALL. You will encounter hurdles in life, but the beautiful thing to know is that God is faithful and that He will always be with you.

Jesus Himself said, '*My Father! If it is possible, let this cup of suffering be taken away from me. Yet I want your will to be done, not mine.*' **Matthew 26:39** (NLT)

The journey of living out your purpose may cause you to encounter pain and suffering, through loss of a relationship and/or of financial support. You may even be abandoned by those closest to you, but do not forget that God will never abandon you. Amen. The most important thing we can do in life is follow God's will for our life. Only then can we truly be fulfilled and live a life of satisfaction. When times get tough formulate the habit of speaking God's truth (the word) over your life!

Jesus experienced great suffering on His journey to fulfilling His destiny, but He remained loyal to His purpose.

Luke 17:25 *But first he must suffer many things and be rejected by this generation.* (NIV)

Do not give up when you pass through times of discouragement, because what you must remember is that you will always have

God by your side and that He will never leave you or forsake you. I remember organising a women's empowerment event and having only a handful of attendees other than my team. It was disheartening because I felt that I had put so much effort into planning and organising gifts, yet many individuals who said they would turn up never showed up. But I still chose to speak my heart out, and I did not let my disappointment stop me from organising future events. I firmly believe that nothing you do for the Lord is in vain. There is always something to learn from past experiences and we should strive to improve and grow. Keep going and keep doing that which God has called you to do. If you touch one life, that one individual can positively impact the world. What you do for the Lord in faith is enough. Stop beating yourself up because you don't 'feel' that your efforts are successful according to the world's standards. The world's standard of success is usually unattainable; it leaves people burnt out, tired and empty. Whereas when you live to please God instead of human beings you gain a sense of peace.

A common obstacle

One of the biggest potential obstacles to your personal progress is your own thought process. Your own views and beliefs about yourself can hold you in bondage. You must allow the Holy Spirit to free your mind through believing God's written and spoken truths (word) concerning your life. Knowing the truth will set you free, and those the Son of God sets free are free indeed.

John 8:31-32 *To the Jews who had believed him, Jesus said, "If you hold to my teaching, you are really my disciples. Then you will know the truth, and the truth will set you free."* (NIV)

If God has given you the go-ahead, then GO AHEAD. Do not let anything or anyone hold you back, for if God is with you who can be against you? As previously mentioned, you do not need to receive a standing ovation from a crowd to accomplish your God-given task. Do not seek the approval of man but rather the approval of God. After all, the human heart is easily swayed. Crowds of people welcomed Christ into Jerusalem with palm trees and shouted, 'Hosanna in the highest', and not long after, multitudes of individuals started shouting crucify Him (Jesus Christ). Don't live to people-please otherwise you will accomplish very little in life.

What you've been called to do by the Lord may not be the 'norm' within society

Deborah was a woman chosen by God to be a judge over the nation of Israel, she was also a prophet. At Barak's request, Deborah, a woman filled with the Holy Spirit, led the Israelite army into battle with the Lord's help. This is simply amazing as it shows that God is willing to use anyone He chooses irrespective of their gender. Hallelujah.

Judges 4:4 *Deborah, the wife of Lappidoth, was a prophet who was judging Israel at that time.* (NLT)

Judges 4:6–10 *One day she sent for Barak son of Abinoam, who lived in Kedesh in the land of Naphtali. She said to him, "This is what the LORD, the God of Israel, commands you: Call out 10,000 warriors from the tribes of Naphtali and Zebulun at Mount Tabor. And I will call out Sisera, commander of Jabin's army, along with his chariots and warriors, to the Kishon River. There I will give you victory over him." Barak told her, "I will go, but only if you go with me." "Very well," she replied, "I will go with you. But you will receive no honor in this venture, for the LORD's victory over Sisera will be at the hands of a woman." So Deborah went with Barak to Kedesh. At Kedesh, Barak called together the tribes of Zebulun and Naphtali, and 10,000 warriors went up with him. Deborah also went with him.* (NLT)

A king at eight years old... Josiah became ruler of a great nation at a very tender age. His right to the throne was not withheld from him because of his age. This tells me that there is no age restriction when it comes to being used by God. Do not let your age hinder you from doing what God has called you to do.

2 Chronicles 34:1 *Josiah was eight years old when he became king, and he reigned in Jerusalem thirty-one years.* (NLT)

Do not compare yourself with others

Galatians 6:4 *Pay careful attention to your own work, for then you will get the satisfaction of a job well done, and you won't need to compare yourself to anyone else.* (NLT)

Your unique life story is meant to be heard by another human being so that they can learn from you! We are like teachers because we possess experiences which others can acquire knowledge from. Therefore, you should not hide within another person's shadow, as you would be robbing another human being of the opportunity to learn and be blessed. Therefore, stop trying to live life in a position or role not meant for you. BE YOURSELF.

We are all on a different journey in life, using different apparatus to help us reach our various destinations. But the most important thing is arriving at the destination which God has set out for us to travel to. Focus on your end goal instead of looking at others; stay in your own lane. When we compare ourselves with others, we end up expressing emotions either of pride or jealously, pride because we may 'feel' that we are superior to another individual, due to believing that we have achieved a lot more, or jealousy because we 'feel' lesser than the person we are comparing ourselves with. And jealousy can potentially lead to wallowing in self-pity, which leads to inactivity and time-wasting. So why be jealous of the person who reaches their destination before you, when they have said that they are on a five-mile journey and your journey is

50 miles? We all have different times and seasons in life – never forget this. God has given us all different tasks and assignments. We have all been created uniquely so we should not expect our lives to follow the same pattern as another human being.

People move at different paces and face different challenges on the way to reaching their destinations. You must be aware of your own potential obstacles, your health needs, emotional needs, physical needs and spiritual needs. Do not let the life of someone else distract you from concentrating on your own work. Everyone has differing needs, so stop trying to copy the methods of others and start following God's blueprint for your life. A good example of contrasting life timings and paces can be seen by looking at the lives of Jacob and Esau.

Genesis 33:12-17 *"Well," Esau said, "let's be going. I will lead the way." But Jacob replied, "You can see, my lord, that some of the children are very young, and the flocks and herds have their young, too. If they are driven too hard, even for one day, all the animals could die. Please, my lord, go ahead of your servant. We will follow slowly, at a pace that is comfortable for the livestock and the children. I will meet you at Seir." "All right," Esau said, "but at least let me assign some of my men to guide and protect you." Jacob responded, "That's not necessary. It's enough that you've received me warmly, my lord!" So Esau turned around and started back to Seir that same day. Jacob, on the other hand, travelled on to Succoth. There he built himself a house and made shelters for his livestock. That is why the place was named Succoth (which means "shelters").* (NLT)

We are all equal in the eyes of God. Therefore, it is useless and meaningless to compare yourself with others. No person is greater than another because of their job or because they have gained more qualifications and achievements compared to those around them. Neither is someone lesser because they do not have a degree. Everyone has a valuable contribution to make within the area in which God has placed them on planet Earth. Picture a multimillion-pound company building. Nobody would be able to use that building if it was not cleaned properly. Therefore, a cleaner is much needed to help keep the environment safe and clean so that others can work in it. Everyone's job role within a business organisation is essential, and should not be looked down upon, regardless of a person's pay grade.

Judges 20:10 *One-tenth of the men from each tribe will be chosen to supply the warriors with food, and the rest of us will take revenge on Gibeah of Benjamin for this shameful thing they have done in Israel.* (NLT)

1 Samuel 30:21-25 *Then David returned to the brook Besor and met up with the 200 men who had been left behind because they were too exhausted to go with him. They went out to meet David and his men, and David greeted them joyfully. But some evil troublemakers among David's men said, "They didn't go with us, so they can't have any of the plunder we recovered. Give them their wives and children, and tell them to be gone." But David said, "No, my brothers! Don't be selfish with what the* LORD *has given us. He has kept us safe and helped us defeat the band of raiders that attacked us. Who will listen when you talk like this? We share and share alike those who go to battle and those who guard the equipment." From then on David made this a decree and regulation for Israel, and it is still followed today.* (NLT)

From the passages above we can see that there is no job role more significant than another. In the book of Judges we can observe that the individuals who prepared meals for the fighting soldiers had just as important a role as those who fought in battle. After all, those who fought needed fuel and energy to do their jobs, and a good nutritious meal would have provided fighting soldiers with much-needed energy. I do not deny the fact that certain roles carry more responsibilities than others, but every role is of value.

You cannot compare an orange with a banana: they are unique and beautiful in their own ways. They have different flavours and benefits. The same goes with people: no two people are the same.

Do not think that because there are several individuals with the same skill as you that you do not need to use and develop your God-given skill. Such a mentality is extremely unhealthy to have! Stop leaving your responsibilities to others because they have a larger following than you do. No person on Earth walks the exact same path in life. Your story is unique, and someone needs to hear YOUR side of things. They need to learn from your specific experiences.

Questions

8) Identify potential obstacles. (Remember you can avoid obstacles by improving in areas which need further development in your life.)

   ....
   ....
   ....
   ....
   ....
   ....
   ....
   ....
   ....
   ....

9) Handwrite your personal **VISION STATEMENT** (a declaration of your objectives that will help assist you in decision making. This is in addition to relying upon the Holy Spirit!).

10) How can you actively and practically grow into the person God created you to be?

11) Can you sum up your goal/purpose in a few words?

....
....
....
....
....
....
....
....
....
....
....
....
....
....
....

12) Can you sum up your goal by using art (e.g. create a logo)?

Extra writing space can be found in the appendix

Take note from Christ

Even though Jesus is King of all kings, He knew what His role on Earth was. He came to serve and not to be served. He did not come to Earth to Lord it over people, but to save the world from sin through His death on the cross and His resurrection.

John 6:15 *When Jesus saw that they were ready to force him to be their king, he slipped away into the hills by himself.* (NLT)

Matthew 20:28 *For even the Son of Man came not to be served but to serve others and to give his life as a ransom for many.* (NLT)

Philippians 2:7 *Instead, he gave up his divine privileges he took the humble position of a slave and was born as a human being. When he appeared in human form.* (NLT)

Do not allow fear to hold you back

Fear of failure can be a huge achievement blocker for many people. Feelings of fear can be paralysing and can prevent individuals from taking a leap of faith. Sadly, this results in many great ideas staying as ideas, but we must realise that fear is not of God. The Lord has not given us the spirit of fear but offers us all sound minds (**2 Timothy 1:7**). A sound mind is a mind capable of healthy and positive thinking. So, choose to meditate on things which are true, pure, lovely, etc.

Philippians 4:8 *Finally, brothers and sisters, whatever is true, whatever is noble, whatever is right, whatever is pure, whatever is lovely, whatever is admirable if anything is excellent or praiseworthy think about such things.* (NIV)

Do not give up just because something does not work out on the first attempt. Just change your method in order to reach your goal. You can fail your way to success. The truth is that some goals take longer to achieve; this is just life. So, keep on working hard and do not lose hope.

Habakkuk 2:3 *This vision is for a future time. It describes the end, and it will be fulfilled. If it seems slow in coming, wait patiently, for it will surely take place. It will not be delayed.* (NLT)

Failing at a task does not make you a failure. You will not be the first person to encounter lack of success in a particular area, nor will you be the last.

Judges 1:21 *The tribe of Benjamin, however, failed to drive out the Jebusites, who were living in Jerusalem. So to this day the Jebusites live in Jerusalem among the people of Benjamin.* (NLT)

Judges 1:30–31 *The tribe of Zebulun failed to drive out the residents of Kitron and Nahalol, so the Canaanites continued to live among them. But the Canaanites were forced to work as slaves for the people of Zebulun. The tribe of Asher failed to drive out the residents of Acco, Sidon, Ahlab, Aczib, Helbah, Aphik, and Rehob.* (NLT)

Sin

Sometimes sin can block your progress. What is the motive behind what you are doing? Is it self-glory, fame, recognition, or do you live to bring glory to God? Are you trying to do things your way or God's way? These are just some great questions to ask yourself and to take into consideration. It is pleasant to see dreams come true but living in disobedience can hinder such happenings.

Proverbs 13:19 *It is pleasant to see dreams come true, but fools refuse to turn from evil to attain them.* (NLT)

Become more open to your artistic side. Explore it, develop it, and grow it through experimentation. Colour, draw, paint, etc.

A moment to pause... Take some time to colour in the shapes in Figure 1 to help you relax.

Figure 1

Continually review your strategy

We cannot always use yesterday's tactics to tackle today's problems. Understand that seasons change, which is why it is always important to ask God about how we ought to handle matters (how we are to manage accomplishing our God-given responsibilities)! Even though David was an experienced man of war he would always ask God how he ought to go about engaging in warfare!

1 Samuel 23:4 *Once again David inquired of the* LORD, *and the* LORD *answered him, "Go down to Keilah, for I am going to give the Philistines into your hand."* (NIV)

1 Samuel 30:8 *Then David asked the LORD, "Should I chase after this band of raiders? Will I catch them?" And the LORD told him, "Yes, go after them. You will surely recover everything that was taken from you!"* (NLT)

2 Samuel 5:19 *So David asked the LORD, "Should I go out to fight the Philistines? Will you hand them over to me?" The LORD replied to David, "Yes, go ahead. I will certainly hand them over to you."* (NLT)

Be aware that at any point in time your conditions may change on your journey to fulfilling your God-given purpose. Therefore, it is essential to be in tune with the Holy Spirit who will alert you to potential dangers ahead, so that you do not feel discouraged or give up on your journey (race of life). Seasons change but God's word concerning your life remains the same, therefore your purpose on Earth remains the same regardless of the difficulties or resistance you may face along the way.

Luke 22:35–36 *Then Jesus asked them, "When I sent you without purse, bag or sandals, did you lack anything?" "Nothing," they answered. He said to them, "But now if you have a purse, take it, and also a bag; and if you don't have a sword, sell your cloak and buy one.* (NLT)

Do not let minimal finances and/or resources stop you

I urge you not to allow lack of funding to be the reason as to why you do not accomplish your God-given tasks! We serve a God who created rivers in the wilderness, so have faith that He will supply ALL your needs. So, if He sends you out, go! For He has already placed within you all you need to achieve, for it is through the Spirit at work within you that you will be able to do ALL things. And if you find yourself in need of more resources He will make a way where there seems to be no way, at the appointed time. He will bring destiny helpers across your path, if it is part of His will for your life, so do not fret. Use what you have and do not despise it. David had a sling and a couple of stones, and this along with faith in God Almighty was enough to defeat Goliath. In the case of Moses, his resource was a shepherd's staff. This very staff transformed into a snake and was held over the Red Sea when it was parted. We must realise that it is not about the resources we have or how much money we own, but about the one who sent us. And God's promise to His children is that He will never leave our side and neither will He forsake us. It is because we have God that we can do exploits. So I urge you to use the resources that God has placed around you and maximise what you have.

1 Samuel 17:40 *He picked up five smooth stones from a stream and put them into his shepherd's bag. Then, armed only with his shepherd's staff and sling, he started across the valley to fight the Philistine.* (NLT)

1 Samuel 17:50 *So David triumphed over the Philistine with only a sling and a stone, for he had no sword.* (NLT)

Exodus 4:1–4 *But Moses protested again, "What if they won't believe me or listen to me? What if they say, 'The LORD never appeared to you'?" Then the LORD asked him, "What is that in your hand?" "A shepherd's staff," Moses replied. "Throw it down on the ground," the LORD told him. So Moses threw down the staff, and it turned into a snake! Moses jumped back. Then the LORD told him, "Reach out and grab its tail." So Moses reached out and grabbed it, and it turned back into a shepherd's staff in his hand.* (NLT)

Exodus 4:20 *So Moses took his wife and sons, put them on a donkey, and headed back to the land of Egypt. In his hand he carried the staff of God.* (NLT)

Using myself as an example, I can truthfully inform you that I did not use an expensive laptop to write this book, the original draft was written on my iPhone notes app. I wrote during my work breaks, and during random moments in the bathroom. I also scheduled a few hours on Saturday afternoons to further develop my work. So be wise in your budgeting, as you do not need to go overboard. Use what you have and purchase what you need.

Do not do things to people-please or to be seen

Do things because you are led by the Holy Spirit, and not because you want to be noticed by others. Never forget that you are noticed by God and that is all that truly matters.

I cannot emphasise this enough, but do not do what you do for numbers. Do it because you're led by the Spirit who has instilled such a passion within you. Even if you touch ONE life it is enough to change the whole world. See it to be a bit like a domino effect, as the encouraged individual has the potential to impact one life or many lives. Do not forget that you may have silent watchers who benefit from what you do. They absorb your content but may be uncomfortable with telling you that you are doing a good job or may assume that you do not need their support or encouragement, because you are getting it elsewhere.

You will have known and UNKNOWN supporters, registered and unregistered subscribers, so never lose heart. Your secret watchers may potentially outnumber those who openly or publicly support you. My personal testimony took place at Lidl, when I bumped into an old acquaintance whom I had not seen in years. She stated that my website was good, which threw me off completely and got me thinking *What website?* I then realised that she was referring to my WordPress blog, which I frequently post on my WhatsApp story to encourage others along their journey of faith. This was very uplifting for me to hear, as I never realised that people clicked on the links which I posted. So keep on doing what God has called you to do, even if you 'feel' no one is benefiting, as your feelings do not always reflect reality. Truth be told, I may never have known that my old-time acquaintance had viewed my content if we never met in Lidl. I believe that the encounter I had was God's way of cheering me on and telling me to keep running my race well.

Another reality you must come to terms with is that in some cases your name will not be known by many or your work may only be recognised by a few. This is ok. It is ok because you should know WHY you do what you do. You do what you do because God has called you to do it and has instilled a specific and unique passion in you, which no one else can fulfil. You do it for God, not for man. A small following on social media does not make your work meaningless. Just because you are not noticed does not make what you do useless. Take for example the human body. It is made up of different organs which contribute to keeping it functioning. Just because I cannot see my thyroid does not in any way mean that my thyroid is unimportant.

Judges 9:52–53 *Abimelek went to the tower and attacked it. But as he approached the entrance to the tower to set it on fire, a woman dropped an upper millstone on his head and cracked his skull.* (NLT)

From the passage above we see that an UNNAMED woman helped prevent her community from being mass murdered. She helped her community gain victory, yet her name went down unknown in history.

We also have an example of another unknown individual in the Bible, from a place called Tekoa. This great woman was known for her wisdom and was asked to help bring about reconciliation between King David and his son Absalom. She was inspired by the Holy Spirit, and I believe that her message was twofold, as part of the message foretold Christ's salvation plan for the world. Christ brings us back to life from spiritual death, through His death and resurrection. Through His life sacrifice the free gift of salvation became available for all. Through the shedding of Christ's blood there is forgiveness of sin.

2 Samuel 14:1–2 *Joab realized how much the king longed to see Absalom. So, he sent for a woman from Tekoa who had a reputation for great wisdom. He said to her, "Pretend you are in mourning; wear mourning clothes and don't put on lotions. Act like a woman who has been mourning for the dead for a long time.* (NLT)

(vs 12–14) *"Please allow me to ask one more thing of my lord the king," she said. "Go ahead and speak," he responded. She replied, "Why don't you do as much for the people of God as you have promised to do for me? You have convicted yourself in making this decision, because you have refused to bring home your own banished son. All of us must die eventually. Our lives are like water spilled out on the ground, which cannot be gathered up again. But God does not just sweep life away; instead, he devises ways to bring us back when we have been separated from him.* (NLT)

A snippet of my life

It was A level results day, and I was on a family holiday in Nigeria. Logging into my UCAS account I discovered that I had not got into the university of my choice. However, I was accepted by my insurance university. My family started to congratulate me and my auntie and uncle seemed to have such joyous smiles on their faces. In all honesty the news made my heart sink, especially since I did not even bother to apply for accommodation at the university I was accepted into, so I then had housing issues to think about. But what I must say is that I trusted God and knew that there was a reason why this was happening.

Three years later, in 2014, I ended up graduating with a 2:2 classification in diagnostic radiography and imaging. I was not thrilled with my result but I was relieved at the fact that I did not have to go through the hassle of doing resits. Before I officially received my degree qualification I was offered a job. I was ecstatic, because this was the first and only job interview which I had attended. It was a great blessing, and I knew that this specific hospital was the place in which I was meant to be, as the interview date and job offer were both on the days on which I fasted. I know that there are many individuals who look down on a 2:2 degree classification, but honestly speaking, in this life it is not always about what you know but WHO you know. And I know the CEO of the universe and His name is God. I am where I am today through His grace alone. I thought I would have to go through the process of attending multiple interviews before securing a job, but God provided for me even before my degree classification was officially awarded.

I have always had a passion for uplifting women and encouraging others, and it was towards the end of 2017 that the Lord motivated me to organise women-empowerment gatherings, called 'Loved Females With Purpose'. I want to convince every reader not to believe the lie that you can only have ONE skill. God has gifted some individuals with the ability to be skilled within many fields, and this is not an unusual phenomenon. While being in full-time employment, working 8.30am–5pm, night shifts, and long days, I was able to complete a level 3 diploma in counselling. This diploma has helped enhance my standard of care for patients by increasing my empathy levels. I have also managed to create regular content for a blog called *Christian Lady After God's Own Heart* aka *CLAGOH*, and have been doing so since September 2014 thanks to the precious grace of God. Once you develop the art of time management you will be able to give an adequate amount of attention to each area of development in your life. When you learn to govern your time effectively you will have time for other essential activities.

There are examples of multi-skilled individuals in the Bible who did not let the opinions of others hinder them from being all that God called them to be. These are real-life stories written in the Bible to encourage us to keep going and to keep trusting in God. King David was a skilled shepherd, harpist, poet, song writer, king and warrior, and a father. Moses was a leader, prophet, song writer and father. David and Moses both faced hardships and made mistakes, yet they both managed to accomplish their purposes on Earth. They were seen as honourable men in the eyes of God. Deborah was the first and only female judge in Israel. She was also a wife, prophet and song writer. So if God says that you can do it, then you can. Have faith and believe.

Deborah

Judges 4:4 *Deborah, the wife of Lappidoth, was a prophet who was judging Israel at that time.* (NLT)

Judges 5:1 *On that day Deborah and Barak son of Abinoam sang this song.* (NLT)

Moses

Deuteronomy 34:10 *There has never been another prophet in Israel like Moses, whom the LORD knew face to face.* (NLT)

Deuteronomy 32:44 *So Moses came with Joshua the son of Nun and spoke all the words of this song in the hearing of the people.* (NKJV)

Exodus 2:21–22 *Moses agreed to stay with the man, who gave his daughter Zipporah to Moses in marriage. Zipporah gave birth to a son, and Moses named him Gershom, saying, "I have become a foreigner in a foreign land.* (NIV)

Exodus 33:12 *Moses said to the Lord, "You have been telling me, 'Lead these people,' but you have not let me know whom you will send with me. You have said, 'I know you by name and you have found favour with me.'* (NIV)

David

1 Samuel 17:12–15 *Now David was the son of an Ephrathite named Jesse, who was from Bethlehem in Judah. Jesse had eight sons, and in Saul's time he was very old. Jesse's three oldest sons had followed Saul to the war: The firstborn was*

Eliab; the second, Abinadab; and the third, Shammah. David was the youngest. The three oldest followed Saul, but David went back and forth from Saul to tend his father's sheep at Bethlehem. (NIV)

2 Samuel 5:4 *David was thirty years old when he became king, and he reigned forty years.* (NIV)

1 Chronicles 3:1 *These are the sons of David who were born in Hebron: ...* (NLT)

1 Samuel 16:18 *Then one of the servants answered and said, "Look, I have seen a son of Jesse the Bethlehemite, who is skillful in playing, a mighty man of valor, a man of war, prudent in speech, and a handsome person, and the Lord is with him."* (NLT)

Also, the book of Psalms is filled with songs and poems which were written by David throughout his lifetime, many of which were written during his moments of hardship. So, don't let the challenges which you face stop you from achieving greatness.

I would like to emphasise that it is the Lord who makes our efforts successful. He will lead us to the right place at the right time, in order to make the right connections with the right people. Trust His timing and His process. And do not forget that you have a part to play, for faith without works is dead. Do not give room to laziness or procrastination as this will hinder your progress.

Psalm 90:17 *And may the Lord our God show us his approval and make our efforts successful. Yes, make our efforts successful!* (NLT)

Stay loyal to your purpose crossword

Across

1 A person whom one has a bond of mutual affection with
4 A feeling of great pleasure
6 The reason you were created
10 Plan the future with great wisdom and imagination
11 Instructions from this book will guide you through life, it is the truth.
12 Firm belief in the reliability of someone or something
14 A group of people bonded by love or blood

Down

2 The ability not to give up
3 Once there is life there is...
5 The Saviour of the world
7 A blissful state of mind regardless of circumstance
8 We all need this type of assistance at some point
9 Makes the world go round
13 Is of the essence

Answers to the crossword can be found in the appendix.

Some advice and important reminders (golden nuggets)

- Always be thankful, as a thankful heart is pleasing to the Lord. Having a heart of gratitude can also help uplift a person's mood for the better.
- Learn to celebrate your small achievements. I believe that many people can accomplish a task a day. Whether it is big or small, a task achieved is a task achieved. Also practise telling yourself well done more often.
- Learn to give! Aspire to invest in the life of others, and I am not just speaking from a financial perspective. We can give our time and energy, as well as our love, to others. The Bible encourages us to be cheerful givers. Formulating the habit of being a blessing unto others is truly a life well spent. You end up reaping joy from the joy you sow into the heart of another.
- Learn to differentiate between healthy, constructive criticism and toxic criticism. You must filter out the junk. This can be achieved through the help and guidance of the Holy Spirit. Beware of people who live to point out faults. They tend to be critical and never have any positive or edifying words to say. They tend to always look for an opportunity to trip you up and destroy your work. Jesus also experienced such an encounter when His disciple Judas betrayed Him.

Luke 22:6 *So he agreed and began looking for an opportunity to betray Jesus so they could arrest him when the crowds weren't around.* (NLT)

- Do not lean on your own understanding, but instead learn to trust in and depend upon God. This is because there may be a way which seems right but ends in destruction. Our feelings can sometimes distort reality, and just because we may experience opposition on our journey to fulfilling our purpose, does not mean that we should give up just because our emotions tell us to. We must keep going and trust God's plan for our lives.
- Be disciplined and stay organised. An important fact which we must remember is that when we lose a day we can never get it back. We may lose money, but lost money can be recovered, whereas yesterday's opportunities are gone forever with yesterday. Be very careful and do not become someone who is lazy and procrastinates often, as there are some opportunities which do not come twice. Moses prayed to The Lord to teach him to understand that life on Earth is brief, and to help him acknowledge the importance of making the right choices with the time he was given. Being disciplined is part of self-love.

Psalm 90:12 *Teach us to realize the brevity of life, so that we may grow in wisdom.* (NLT)

Proverbs 13:24 *Those who spare the rod of discipline hate their children. Those who love their children care enough to discipline them.* (NLT)

- God's word is never out of date. His word is always in season and NEVER out of season. Let God's word be your guide, for it will help you and inspire you.

- Stay prayed up as this will help protect your mind against negativity and the lies of Satan. Choose to believe God's written truth about you instead of the devil's lies and accusations against you.
- Do NOT neglect personal time with God. Once in a while it is necessary to get away from the noise and busyness of this world and enjoy time in seclusion with the Maker of the universe. Set aside time each day for fellowship (communication) with the King of all kings.
- HAVE FUN! Enjoy what you do instead of seeing it as a chore, otherwise you will quickly lose motivation! Strive to do things with enthusiasm.

Romans 12:11 *Never be lazy, but work hard and serve the Lord enthusiastically.* (NLT)

- Surround yourself with like-minded individuals who will impart wisdom into you – individuals who will support and encourage you.

Proverbs 13:20 *Walk with the wise and become wise, associate with fools and get in trouble.* (NLT)

- Love yourself and learn to watch your thoughts, as your own thoughts have the power to hold you in bondage (believing the lies of the devil can hold you down).

God's word is never out of

date, always in season,

NEVER *out of season.*

- Learn to say no. There will be times when you will need to say no, so that you do not run yourself into the ground and end up exhausted. It is also necessary to say no without fear when asked to do something against your conscience. Saying no can help you save time and can help you avoid getting into hurtful/manipulative partnerships. Remember, not all opportunities and potential partnerships/collaborations are beneficial, so choose wisely the activities in which you partake. Remember, too much activity can negatively impact your health.

Ecclesiastes 5:3 *Too much activity gives you restless dreams, too many words make you a fool.* (NLT)

- Before launching into a project DO YOUR RESEARCH. This is so that you know the steps which need to be taken to fulfil your purpose, as well as the resources needed.

Joshua 18:8 *As the men started on their way to map out the land, Joshua commanded them, "Go and explore the land and write a description of it. Then return to me, and I will assign the land to the tribes by casting sacred lots here in the presence of the LORD at Shiloh."* (NLT)

- There is a lesson to be learnt in all situations, whether good or bad, favourable, or unfavourable. Always remember the Lord will turn around for good what Satan intended for evil, therefore always be willing to learn from your experiences.

There is a lesson to be learnt in all situations, whether good or bad, favourable, or unfavourable.

- Learn to accept wise counsel (healthy, constructive criticism).

Proverbs 13:18 *If you ignore criticism, you will end in poverty and disgrace; if you accept correction, you will be honoured.* (NLT)

- You cannot do everything on your own, you will always need the help of others throughout life. You must know that God will touch the hearts of those He has called to assist you on the journey to fulfilling your destiny.

1 Samuel 10:24–26 *Then Samuel said to all the people, "This is the man the LORD has chosen as your king. No one in all Israel is like him!" And all the people shouted, "Long live the king!" Then Samuel told the people what the rights and duties of a king were. He wrote them down on a scroll and placed it before the LORD. Then Samuel sent the people home again. When Saul returned to his home at Gibeah, a group of men whose hearts God had touched went with him.* (NLT)

- If you find that you frequently forget to do scheduled tasks, set appropriate reminders on your phone. More often than not, most people tend to carry their phones around with them wherever they go. So, instead of wasting your time getting distracted on social media apps, or prying on other people's lives, use your mobile phone to your advantage. Set reminders, write up notes and organise meetings, etc.
- Develop a purposeful mindset and be intentional about what you do. In all you do work towards achieving your God-given purpose while bringing glory to God in the process.

1 Corinthians 9:26 *So I run with purpose in every step. I am not just shadowboxing.* (NLT)

With every step you take, step

WITH *purpose,* ON *purpose*

and INTO *purpose.*

How to manage your time

When embarking on a project it is important that you do not neglect yourself, your family or God. Work life balance is very important and as mentioned earlier lost time cannot be regained. Strive to spend quality time with your family and do not get so caught up in working on a project to the point at which you forget everything else exists. Do not neglect those who you love.

The Bible requires for believers to love the Lord with all their heart, therefore as Christians we ought not to allow anything to take God's place in our lives. Not even our ministry work should come before The Lord. Let God be God in your life and do not confuse ministry time with your alone-time with God.

Seek to set realistic time frames so that you create quality work instead of producing inadequate produce, due to rushing to meet a deadline. If you set a timeframe of four weeks use the WHOLE four weeks. Avoid arriving at week three and then deciding that it is time to get working, as you will have robbed yourself of precious time. A day gone is a day you can never get back and each day comes with fresh opportunities.

If you have set aside three hours to work on your purpose, try to stick to it and set a timer if necessary. This can help prevent burnout due to overworking. It is also a good method to use to prevent your work from infringing on your family time, as well as time needed for other activities or responsibilities you may have. Take breaks in between the hours you have committed to working, so that you do not exhaust yourself. I would suggest a five- to 10-minute break every one to 1.5 hours. Also take a day off during the week for respite; human bodies NEED adequate rest to function properly. Remember you are not a machine and even machines need to be turned off occasionally, otherwise they malfunction. Look after your body as both your physical and mental health are extremely important, and a key to producing quality work is taking quality care of yourself.

Use free moments (periods of downtime) when at work to work on external projects. Even if you labour for just five minutes it all adds up. Five minutes every day for a year adds up to 30.41 hours – more than one full day of work. And if you really want to you can use five minutes of your lunchbreak to work on external tasks. Just ensure that you give yourself enough time to rest. If you use your time well, more opportunities will be given to you to further use your time effectively.

Luke 19:26 "*Yes,' the king replied, 'and to those who use well what they are given, even more will be given. But from those who do nothing, even what little they have will be taken away.* (NLT)

SUNDAY	MONDAY	TUESDAY	WEDNESDAY	THURSDAY	FRIDAY	SATURDAY
1 Meditate on Philippians 4:8.	2 Call someone to check on how they are doing.	3 Write a gratitude list.	4 Go for a long walk.	5 Do a crossword.	6 Have a nice, sweet treat.	7 Visit a local park.
8 Host someone or a group.	9 Hold the door open for someone.	10 Study the Bible with someone.	11 Write a journal.	12 Make a smoothie.	13 Meet up with a friend.	14 Bake a cake.
15 Create a vision board.	16 Make a colleague smile.	17 Dance, be free, and workout.	18 Write a creative piece (poem or song).	19 Pray for someone.	20 Join a Bible study group.	21 Listen to uplifting songs (e.g., songs of praise).
22 Play a game.	23 Explore a new hobby.	24 Cook a new recipe.	25 Explore painting.	26 Try a new workout.	27 Pamper yourself with a facial and a warm refreshing drink.	28 Network (maybe attend an event).
29 Sign up for a course which will enhance your personal development.	30 Send out an encouraging text message.	31 Think of ways to further deepen your relationship with God.				

Just an example of how you can manage your mental, physical and spiritual health effectively by staying proactive. This can also help prevent you from throwing yourself a pity party. We should strive to enjoy the time which God has given us on Earth.

Ending

Remember that with Christ's help you can do ALL things in line with HIS will for your life.

Philippians 4:13 *For I can do everything through Christ, who gives me strength.* (NLT)

Psalm 73:24 *You guide me with your counsel, leading me to a glorious destiny.* (NLT)

Do you want to accept Christ?

A prayer of salvation

Accept that you are a sinner.

Believe in the Lord Jesus Christ. Believe that He came into the world to redeem mankind, and that He died in your place and rose again on the third day. Trust that His precious blood has the power to cleanse you of all your sins once you ask for His forgiveness.

Commit yourself and all your ways to the Lord and live a life of total surrender to Him.

If you would like support on your journey of faith, do try to locate a Bible-believing church or contact clagoh@outlook.com for prayers, encouragement and/or advice.

God bless.

About the author

Mary-Ann was born and raised in England and currently lives with her parents and two younger sisters. She presently works as a radiographer and loves to bake, blog, pursue healthy living, study scripture daily and travel during her free time. But in summary, she is a woman saved by grace, a child of God and loves God. Mary-Ann is on a continual journey of getting to know The Lord more deeply every passing day.

Appendix

Crossword answers

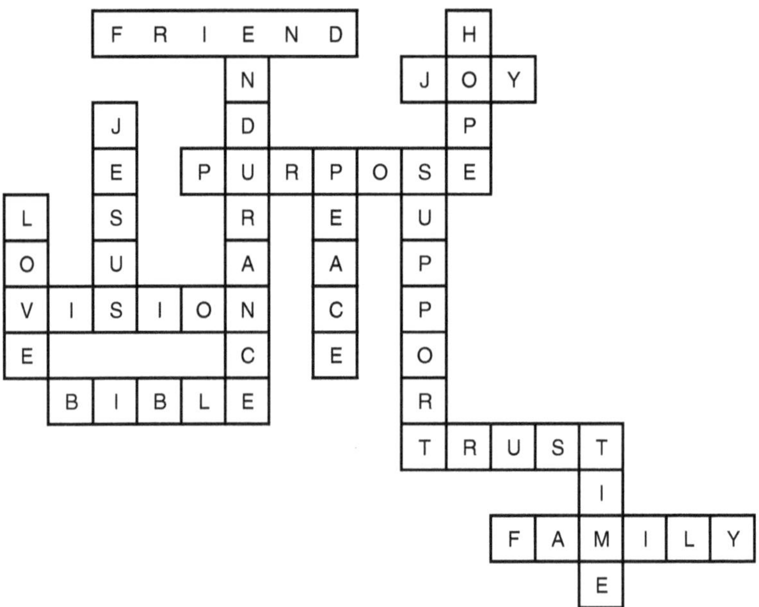

A list of resources

1) **'Christian Lady After God's Own Heart':** A platform on which you can access free Bible-inspired advice via WordPress. There you will find inspirational posts created to encourage and inspire human minds through using the Bible. ChristianLadyAfterGodsOwnHeart.co.uk
2) **Canva:** A graphic design platform which enables users to create their own logos, posters, social media images and other visual content. Many of these resources can be downloaded for free. There is a charge for some.
3) **Pixabay:** Get your hands on images which you can download for free with no attribution required (free for commercial use).
4) **Eventbrite:** Create and promote your own event completely free of charge using the Eventbrite platform. Events which require the purchase of a paid ticket will result in an admin fee.
5) **AIM GROUP:** Have you ever thought about doing an apprenticeship? Does the chance of getting paid while you learn interest you? If so, check out the AIM GROUP, an organisation which specialises in finding training and employment opportunities for those with the desire to live up to their full potential.
6) **WordPress:** Create your own free website or build a blog with ease. WordPress has dozens of free customisable mobile-ready designs and themes, as well as free hosting.
7) **One Year Bible Online:** Access different Bible-reading plans free of charge. This platform helps individuals who are seeking to read the Bible in a year.
8) **YouTube:** Watch tutorials free of charge and/or promote your work.
9) **UCAS apprenticeships:** This organisation connects people to post-university studies, including teacher

training, apprenticeships and internships. Work and learn at the same time while having your course fee covered by your employer.

10) **Unsplash:** A website which provides free high-resolution images.

An additional nugget

<u>We all have what it takes to be an influencer!</u>

We all have a God-given purpose, which is to bring The Lord glory through the way that we live and to honour Him with the resources we have. We all have the ability through the power of the Holy Spirit to influence others to do good. You can uplift and inspire others by sharing your life story.

Jeremiah 15:19 *"This is how the Lord responds: "If you return to me, I will restore you so you can continue to serve me. If you speak good words rather than worthless ones, you will be my spokesman.* ***You must influence them;*** *do not let them influence you!"* (NLT)

Whether you be a baker, personal trainer or a designer, whatever you do, do it for the glory of God. Your godly, sweet and gentle attitude can positively inspire those you meet and encourage them to do better. Seeing another human being overcome a tough life challenge can bring other individuals hope. To further explain myself, picture an individual who has lost a drastic amount of weight due to making positive and healthy lifestyle choices. Their actions can potentially motivate and move others to do the same. Also, hearing someone attribute their success to God can cause some individuals to want to discover more about that person's relationship with God. You can be used by God to draw more people into His kingdom, through your everyday job! You do not have to be a preacher to be able to do this!

We have a biblical example of this when we look at the life of an ordinary woman described in the book of John, who pointed people to Christ through using word of mouth.

John 4:7–26 *"Soon a Samaritan woman came to draw water, and Jesus said to her, "Please give me a drink." He was alone at the time because his disciples had gone into the village to buy some food. The woman was surprised, for Jews refuse to have anything to do with Samaritans. She said to Jesus, "You are a Jew, and I am a Samaritan woman. Why are you asking me for a drink?" Jesus replied, "If you only knew the gift God has for you and who you are speaking to, you would ask me, and I would give you living water." "But sir, you don't have a rope or a bucket," she said, "and this well is very deep. Where would you get this living water? And besides, do you think you're greater than our ancestor Jacob, who gave us this well? How can you offer better water than he and his sons and his animals enjoyed?" Jesus replied, "Anyone who drinks this water will soon become thirsty again. But those who drink the water I give will never be thirsty again. It becomes a fresh, bubbling spring within them, giving them eternal life." "Please, sir," the woman said, "give me this water! Then I'll never be thirsty again, and I won't have to come here to get water." "Go and get your husband," Jesus told her. "I don't have a husband," the woman replied. Jesus said, "You're right! You don't have a husband for you have had five husbands, and you aren't even married to the man you're living with now. You certainly spoke the truth!" "Sir," the woman said, "you must be a prophet. So tell me, why is it that you Jews insist that Jerusalem is the only place of worship, while we Samaritans claim it is here at Mount Gerizim, where our ancestors worshiped?" Jesus replied, "Believe me, dear woman, the time is coming when it will no longer matter whether you worship the Father on this mountain or in Jerusalem. You Samaritans know very little about the one you worship, while we Jews know all about him, for salvation* *comes through the Jews. But the time is coming indeed it's here now when true worshipers will worship the Father in spirit and in truth. The Father is looking for those who will worship him that way. For God is Spirit, so those who worship him must worship in spirit and in truth." The woman said, "I know the Messiah is coming the one who is called Christ. When he comes, he will explain everything to us." Then Jesus told her, " I AM the Messiah!" (NLT)*

John 4: 28–30 *The woman left her water jar beside the well and ran back to the village, telling everyone, "Come and see a man who told me everything I ever did! Could he possibly be the Messiah?" So the people came streaming from the village to see him.* (NLT)

John 4:39 *Many Samaritans from the village believed in Jesus because the woman had said, "He told me everything I ever did!"* (NLT)

This woman had a bad reputation within her community due to having five previous husbands and living with a man she was not married to. She wasn't an Old Testament scholar yet her testimony of her encounter with Christ led to a whole community hearing the truth and caused many to receive and accept Christ. Now, she wasn't perfect, just as none of us are, but even so her testimony turned people to the Messiah.

Likewise, Christians should aspire to turn others to Christ through the way in which they live! Before we accepted God's precious gift of salvation we may have lived in an ungodly and repulsive manner (a lifestyle dominated by sin), but now that we have Christ our lives should bring Him glory (change for the better).

You have been given an assignment by Christ, therefore, stop neglecting your duty to influence others for the better. It is either you influence others to do good OR evil... Or they influence you! You have the ability to influence, you are an influencer in your own right, in your own unique and special way.

God bless

x

Notes

Notes

Notes

Notes

Notes

www.ingramcontent.com/pod-product-compliance
Lightning Source LLC
LaVergne TN
LVHW052348100826
845147LV00012B/784

9781839759970